Preparation for Total Consecration
according to
Saint Louis de Montfort

W9-BYF-030

Montfort Publications
Bay Shore, New York

IMPRIMI POTEST:
>   Frank Setzer, S.M.M.
>   *Provincial Superior*

NIHIL OBSTAT:
>   William F. Hughes, S.T.L.
>   *Censor Librorum*

IMPRIMATUR:
>   Walter Philip Kellenberg, D.D.
>   *Bishop of Rockville Centre*

Fifteenth Printing, 2000 - 25,000

ISBN 0-910984-10-7

Cover: Designed by Christine Micciche

Statuary Group of Mary Queen of All
Hearts by Gerard Ouellet, S.M.M.

Photo: Rev. Maurice Therriault, S.M.M.

INTRODUCTION

St. Louis de Montfort tells us that "those who desire to take up this special devotion" (Total Consecration to Jesus Through Mary), "should spend at least twelve days in emptying themselves of the spirit of the world, which is opposed to the spirit of Jesus. They should spend three weeks imbuing themselves with the spirit of Jesus through the most Blessed Virgin." (T.D. No. 227)

It is obvious that this total consecration, or perfect renewal of our baptismal vows with and through Mary, is not to be taken lightly. Pope John Paul II said that "Reading this book (St. Louis de Montfort's *True Devotion to Mary*) was to be a turning point in my life ... This Marian devotion ... has since remained a part of me. It is an integral part of my interior life and of my spiritual theology." In his Marian Year encyclical, *Mother of the Redeemer*, speaking of *Marian Spirituality*, the Holy Father singles out: "among the many witnesses of this spirituality, the figure of Saint Louis Marie Grignion de Montfort, who proposes consecration to Christ through the hands of Mary, as an effective means for Christians to live faithfully their baptismal commitments." (No. 48)

This booklet is intended merely as a guide to help you in your immediate preparation before entering fully into this beautiful way of Marian Spirituality, in the footsteps of her Son, Jesus.

– *The Editors*

DAILY EXERCISES
SIX SUGGESTED SCHEDULES FOR CONSECRATION
Part I: (12 Days) *Spirit of the World*

	I	II	III	IV	V	VI
1st Day:	Dec. 31	Feb. 20	March 26	April 28	July 13	Nov. 5
2nd Day:	Jan. 1	Feb. 21	March 27	April 29	July 14	Nov. 6
3rd Day:	Jan. 2	Feb. 22	March 28	April 30	July 15	Nov. 7
4th Day:	Jan. 3	Feb. 23	March 29	May 1	July 16	Nov. 8
5th Day:	Jan. 4	Feb. 24	March 30	May 2	July 17	Nov. 9
6th Day:	Jan. 5	Feb. 25	March 31	May 3	July 18	Nov. 10
7th Day:	Jan. 6	Feb. 26	April 1	May 4	July 19	Nov. 11
8th Day:	Jan. 7	Feb. 27	April 2	May 5	July 20	Nov. 12
9th Day:	Jan. 8	Feb. 28	April 3	May 6	July 21	Nov. 13
10th Day:	Jan. 9	March 1	April 4	May 7	July 22	Nov. 14
11th Day:	Jan. 10	March 2	April 5	May 8	July 23	Nov. 15
12th Day:	Jan. 11	March 3	April 6	May 9	July 24	Nov. 16

Part II: (1st Week) *Knowledge of Self*

	I	II	III	IV	V	VI
13th Day:	Jan. 12	March 4	April 7	May 10	July 25	Nov. 17
14th Day:	Jan. 13	March 5	April 8	May 11	July 26	Nov. 18
15th Day:	Jan. 14	March 6	April 9	May 12	July 27	Nov. 19
16th Day:	Jan. 15	March 7	April 10	May 13	July 28	Nov. 20
17th Day:	Jan. 16	March 8	April 11	May 14	July 29	Nov. 21
18th Day:	Jan. 17	March 9	April 12	May 15	July 30	Nov. 22
19th Day:	Jan. 18	March 10	April 13	May 16	July 31	Nov. 23

Part III: (2nd Week) *Knowledge of Our Lady*

	I	II	III	IV	V	VI
20th Day:	Jan. 19	March 11	April 14	May 17	August 1	Nov. 24
21st Day:	Jan. 20	March 12	April 15	May 18	August 2	Nov. 25
22nd Day:	Jan. 21	March 13	April 16	May 19	August 3	Nov. 26
23rd Day:	Jan. 22	March 14	April 17	May 20	August 4	Nov. 27
24th Day:	Jan. 23	March 15	April 18	May 21	August 5	Nov. 28
25th Day:	Jan. 24	March 16	April 19	May 22	August 6	Nov. 29
26th Day:	Jan. 25	March 17	April 20	May 23	August 7	Nov. 30

Part IV: (3rd Week) *Knowledge of Christ*

	I	II	III	IV	V	VI
27th Day:	Jan. 26	March 18	April 21	May 24	August 8	Dec. 1
28th Day:	Jan. 27	March 19	April 22	May 25	August 9	Dec. 2
29th Day:	Jan. 28	March 20	April 23	May 26	August 10	Dec. 3
30th Day:	Jan. 29	March 21	April 24	May 27	August 11	Dec. 4
31st Day:	Jan. 30	March 22	April 25	May 28	August 12	Dec. 5
32nd Day:	Jan. 31	March 23	April 26	May 29	August 13	Dec. 6
33rd Day:	Feb. 1	March 24	April 27	May 30	August 14	Dec. 7
Consecration Day	Feb. 2	March 25	April 28	May 31	August 15	Dec. 8

PART I
TWELVE PRELIMINARY DAYS

Theme: SPIRIT OF THE WORLD

xamine your conscience, pray, practice renouncement of your own will; mortification, purity of heart. This purity is the indispensable condition for contemplating God in heaven, to see Him on earth and to know Him by the light of faith.

The first part of the preparation should be employed in casting off the spirit of the world which is contrary to that of Jesus Christ. The spirit of the world consists essentially in the denial of the supreme dominion of God; a denial which is manifested in practice by sin and disobedience; thus it is principally opposed to the spirit of Christ, which is also that of Mary.

It manifests itself by the concupiscence of the flesh, by the concupiscence of the eyes and by the pride of life, by disobedience to God's laws and the abuse of created things. Its works are: sin in all forms, then all else by which the devil leads to sin; works which bring error and darkness to the mind, and seduction and corruption to the will. Its pomps are the splendor and the charms employed by the devil to render sin alluring in persons, places and things.

PRAYERS TO BE RECITED DURING THESE FIRST TWELVE DAYS

Veni Creator

Come, O Creator Spirit blest!
And in our souls take up Thy rest;
Come with Thy grace and heavenly aid,
To fill the hearts which Thou hast made.

Great Paraclete! To Thee we cry,
O highest gift of God most high!
O font of life! O fire of love!
And sweet anointing from above.

Thou in Thy Sevenfold gifts art known,
The finger of God's hand we own;
The promise of the Father, Thou!
Who dost the tongue with power endow.

Kindle our senses from above,
And make our hearts o'erflow with love;
With patience firm and virtue high
The weakness of our flesh supply.

Far from us drive the foe we dread,
And grant us Thy true peace instead;
So shall we not, with Thee for guide,
Turn from the path of life aside.

Oh, may Thy grace on us bestow
The Father and the Son to know,
And Thee through endless times confessed
of both the eternal Spirit blest.

All glory while the ages run
Be to the Father and the Son
Who rose from death; the same to Thee,
O Holy Spirit, eternally. Amen.

Ave Maris Stella

Hail, bright star of ocean,
God's own Mother blest,
Ever sinless Virgin,
Gate of heavenly rest.

Taking that sweet Ave
Which from Gabriel came,
Peace confirm within us,
Changing Eva's name.

Break the captives' fetters,
Light on blindness pour,
All our ills expelling,
Every bliss implore.

Show thyself a Mother;
May the Word Divine,
Born for us thy Infant,
Hear our prayers through thine.

3

Virgin all excelling,
Mildest of the mild,
Freed from guilt, preserve us,
Pure and undefiled.

Keep our life all spotless,
Make our way secure,
Till we find in Jesus
Joy forevermore.

Through the highest heaven
To the Almighty Three,
Father, Son and Spirit,
One same Glory be. Amen.

Magnificat

My Soul doth magnify the Lord.

And my spirit hath rejoiced in God my Savior.

Because He hath regarded the humility of His handmaid; for behold, from henceforth all generations shall call me blessed.

Because He that is mighty hath done great things to me; and holy is His name.

And His mercy is from generation to generations, to them that fear Him.

He hath showed might in His arm; He hath scattered the proud in the conceit of their heart.

He hath put down the mighty from their seat; and hath exalted the humble.

He hath filled the hungry with good things; and

4

the rich he hath sent empty away.

He hath received Israel His servant, being mindful of His mercy.

As He spoke to our fathers, to Abraham and to his seed forever. Amen.

Glory be to the Father, etc.

First Day

St. Matthew: Chapter 5: 1-19

The Beatitudes

Seeing the crowds, he went up the hill. There he sat down and was joined by his disciples. Then he began to speak, This is what he taught them:

How happy are the poor in spirit:
theirs is the kingdom of heaven.
Happy the gentle:
they shall have the earth for their heritage.
Happy those who mourn:
they shall be comforted.
Happy those who hunger and thirst for what is right:
they shall be satisfied.
Happy the merciful:
they shall have mercy shown them.
Happy the pure in heart:
they shall see God.
Happy those who are persecuted in the cause of right:
theirs is the kingdom of heaven.
Happy are you when people abuse you and persecute you and speak all kinds of calumny

5

against you on my account. Rejoice and be glad, for your reward will be great in heaven; this is how they persecuted the prophets before you.

Salt of the earth and light of the world

You are the salt of the earth. But if salt becomes tasteless, what can make it salty again? It is good for nothing and can only be thrown out to be trampled underfoot by men.

You are the light of the world. A city built on a hill-top cannot be hidden. No one lights a lamp to put it under a tub; they put it on the lamp-stand where it shines for everyone in the house. In the same way your light must shine in the sight of men, so that, seeing your good works, they may give the praise to your Father in heaven.

The fulfillment of the Law

Do not imagine that I have come to abolish the Law or the Prophets. I have come not to abolish but to complete them. I tell you solemnly, till heaven and earth disappear, not one dot, not one little stroke, shall disappear from the Law until its purpose is achieved.

Now turn to page 2, For Prayers, etc.

SECOND DAY

St. Matthew: Chapters 5: 48, 6: 1-15

Even the pagans do as much, do they not? You

must therefore be perfect just as your heavenly Father is perfect.

Almsgiving in secret (6: 1-15)
Be careful not to parade your good deeds before men to attract their notice; by doing this you will lose all reward from your Father in heaven. So when you give alms, do not have it trumpeted before you; this is what the hypocrites do in the synagogues and in the streets to win men's admiration. I tell you solemnly, they have had their reward. But when you give alms, your left hand must not know what your right is doing; your almsgiving must be secret, and your Father who sees all that is done in secret will reward you.

Prayer in secret
And when you pray, do not imitate the hypocrites: they love to say their prayers standing up in the synagogues and at the street corners for people to see them. I tell you solemnly, they have had their reward. But when you pray, go to your private room and, when you have shut your door, pray to your Father who is in that secret place, and your father who sees all that is done in secret will reward you.

How to pray. The Lord's Prayer
In your prayers do not babble as the pagans do, for they think that by using many words they will make themselves heard. Do not be like them; your Father knows what you need before you ask him. So you should pray like this:

7

Our Father in heaven,
may your name be held holy,
your kingdom come,
your will be done,
on earth as in heaven.
Give us today our daily bread.
And forgive us our debts,
as we have forgiven those who are in debt to us.
And do not put us to the test,
but save us from the evil one.

Yes, if you forgive others their failings, your heavenly Father will forgive you yours; but if you do not forgive others, your Father will not forgive your failings either.

Now turn to page 2, For Prayers, etc.

Third Day

St. Matthew: Chapter 7: 1-14

Do not judge

Do not judge, and you will not be judged; because the judgements you give are the judgements you will get, and the amount you measure out is the amount you will be given. Why do you observe the splinter in your brother's eye and never notice the plank in your own? How dare you say to your brother, "Let me take the splinter out of your eye", when all the time there is a plank in your own? Hypocrite! Take the plank out of your own eye first, and then you will see clearly enough to take the splinter out of your brother's eye.

Do not profane sacred things
Do not give dogs what is holy; and do not throw your pearls in front of pigs, or they may trample them and then turn on you and tear you to pieces.

Effective prayer
Ask, and it will be given to you; search, and you will find; knock, and the door will be opened to you. For the one who asks always receives; the one who searches always finds; the one who knocks will always have the door opened to him. Is there a man among you who would hand his son a stone when he asked for bread? Or would hand him a snake when he asked for a fish? If you, then, who are evil, know how to give your children what is good, how much more will your Father in heaven give good things to those who ask him!

The golden rule
So always treat others as you would like them to treat you; that is the meaning of the Law and the Prophets.

The two ways
Enter by the narrow gate, since the road that leads to perdition is wide and spacious, and many take it; but it is a narrow gate and a hard road that leads to life, and only a few find it.

Now turn to page 2, For Prayers, etc.

FOURTH DAY

Imitation: Book 3, Chapters 7, 40

That man has no good of himself, and that he cannot glory in anything

Lord, what is man, that Thou art mindful of him; or the son of man, that Thou visit him? What has man deserved that Thou should give him grace? Lord, what cause have I to complain, if Thou forsakest me,or what can I justly allege, if what I petition Thou shalt not grant? This most assuredly, I may truly think and say: Lord I am nothing, I can do nothing of myself, that is good, but I am in all things defective and ever tend to nothing. And unless I am assisted and interiorly instructed by Thee, I become wholly tepid and relaxed, but Thou, O Lord, art always the same, and endure unto eternity, ever good, just and holy, doing all things well, justly and holily and disposing them in wisdom.

But I who am more inclined to go back, than to go forward, continue not always in one state, for I am changed, seven different times. But it quickly becomes better when it pleases Thee, and Thou stretchest out Thy helping hand: for Thou alone, without man's aid can assist me and so strengthen me, that my countenance shall be more diversely changed: but my heart be converted and find its rest in Thee alone.

He who would be too secure in time of peace will often be found too much dejected in time of war. If you could always continue to be humble and little in your own eyes, and keep your spirit in due order and subjection, you would not fall so easily into danger and offense. It is good counsel that, when you have conceived the spirit of fervor, you should meditate how it will be when that light shall be withdrawn.

Now turn to page 2, For Prayers, etc.

FIFTH DAY

Imitation: Continued: Book 3, Chapter 40

Wherefore, but I did know well, how to cast from me all human comfort, either for the sake of devotion, or through the necessity by which I am compelled to seek Thee, because there is no man that can comfort me. Then might I deservedly hope in Thy favor, and rejoice in the gift of a new consolation. Thanks be to Thee from Whom all things proceed, as often as it happens to me, I, indeed, am but vanity and nothing in Thy sight, an inconstant and weak man. Where, therefore, can I glory, or for what do I desire to be thought of highly?

Forsooth of my very nothingness; and this is most vain. Truly vainglory is an evil plague, because it draws away from true glory, and robs us of heavenly grace. For, while a man takes complacency in himself, he displeases Thee; while he looks for human applause, he is deprived of true virtues. But true, glory and holy exultation is to glory in Thee, and not in one's self; to rejoice in Thy Name, but not in one's own strength. To find pleasure in no creature, save only for Thy sake. Let Thy Name be praised, not mine; let Thy work be magnified, not mine; let Thy Holy Name be blessed, but let nothing be attributed to me of the praise of men. Thou art my glory; Thou art the exultation of my heart; in Thee, will I glory and rejoice all the day; but for myself, I will glory in nothing but in my infirmities.

Now turn to page 2, For Prayers, etc.

SIXTH DAY

Imitation: Book 1, Chapter 18

On the examples of the Holy Fathers

Look upon the lively examples of the holy Fathers in whom shone real perfection and the religious life, and you will see how little it is, and almost nothing that we do. Alas, what is our life when we compare it with theirs? Saints and friends of Christ, they served our Lord in hunger and in thirst, in cold, in nakedness, in labor and in weariness, in watching, in fasting, prayers and holy meditations, and in frequent persecutions and reproaches. Oh, how many grievous tribulations did the Apostles suffer and the Martyrs and Confessors and Virgins, and all the rest who resolved to follow the steps of Christ! For they hated their lives in this world, that they might keep them in life everlasting. Oh, what a strict and self-renouncing life the holy Fathers of the desert led! What long and grievous temptations did they bear! How often were they harassed by the enemy, what frequent and fervent prayers did they offer up to God, what rigorous abstinence did they practice!

What a valiant contest waged they to subdue their imperfections! What purity and straight forwardness of purpose kept them towards God! By day they labored, and much of the night they spent in prayer; though while they labored, they were far from leaving off mental prayer, They spent all their time profitably. Every hour seemed short to spend with God; and even their necessary bodily refreshment was forgotten in the great sweetness of contemplation. They renounced all riches, dignities, honors and kindred; they hardly took what was necessary for life. It grieved them to serve the body even in its necessity. Accordingly, they were poor in earthly things, but very rich in grace and virtues.

Now turn to page 2, For Prayers, etc.

SEVENTH DAY

Imitation: Book 1, Chapter 18

Outwardly they suffered want, but within they were refreshed with grace and Divine consolation. They were aliens to the world; they seemed as nothing and the world despised them; but they were precious and beloved in the sight of God. They persevered in true humility, they lived in simple obedience, they walked in charity and patience, and so every day they advanced in spirit and gained great favor with God. They were given for example to all religious, and ought more to excite us to advance in good, than the number of lukewarm to induce us to grow remiss. Oh! how great was the fervor of all religious in the beginning of their holy institute! Oh, how great was their devotion in prayer, how great was their zeal for virtue! How vigorous the discipline that was kept up, what reverence and obedience, under the rule of the superior, flourished in all! Their traces that remain still bear witness, that they were truly holy and perfect men who did battle so stoutly, and trampled the world under their feet. Now, he is thought great who is not a transgressor; and who can, with patience, endure what he has undertaken. Ah, the lukewarmness and negligence of our state! that we soon fall away from our first fervor, and are even now tired with life, from slothfulness and tepidity. Oh, that advancement in virtue be not quite asleep in thee, who hast so often seen the manifold examples of the devout!

Now turn to page 2, For Prayers, etc.

EIGHTH DAY
Imitation: Book 1, Chapter 13

Of resisting temptations

As long as we live in this world, we cannot be without temptations and tribulations. Hence it is written in Job "Man's life on earth is a temptation." Everyone therefore should be solicitous about his temptations and watch in prayer lest the devil find an opportunity to catch him: he who never sleeps, but goes about, seeking whom he can devour. No one is so perfect and holy as sometimes not to have

14

temptations and we can never be wholly free from them. Nevertheless, temptations are very profitable to man, troublesome and grievous though they may be, for in them a man is humbled, purified and instructed. All the Saints passed through many tribulations and temptations and were purified by them. And they that could not support temptations, became reprobate and fell away.

Many seek to flee temptations, and fall worse into them. We cannot conquer by flight alone, but by patience and true humility we become stronger than all our enemies. He who only declines them outwardly, and does not pluck out their root, will profit little; nay, temptations will sooner return and he will find himself in a worse condition. By degrees and by patience you will, by God's grace, better overcome them than by harshness and your own importunity. Take council the oftener in temptation, and do not deal harshly with one who is tempted; but pour in consolation, as you would wish to be done unto yourself. Inconstancy of mind and little confidence in God, is the beginning of all temptations. For as a ship without a helm is driven to and fro by the waves, so the man who neglects and gives up his resolutions is tempted in many ways.

Now turn to page 2, For Prayers, etc.

NINTH DAY

Imitation: Book 1, Chapter 13

Fire tries iron, and temptation a just man. We often know not what we are able to do, but temptations discover what we are. Still, we must watch, especially in the beginning of temptation; for then the enemy is more easily overcome, if he be not suffered to enter the door of the mind, but is withstood upon the threshold the very moment he knocks. Whence a certain one has said "Resist beginnings; all too late the cure." When ills have gathered strength, by long delay, first there comes from the mind a simple thought; then a strong imagination, afterwards delight, and the evil motion and consent and so, little by little the fiend does gain entrance, when he is not resisted in the beginning. The longer anyone has been slothful in resisting, so much the weaker he becomes daily in himself, and the enemy, so much the stronger in him. Some suffer grievous temptations in the beginning of their conversion, others in the end and others are troubled nearly their whole life. Some are very lightly tempted, according to the wisdom and the equity of the ordinance of God who weighs man's conditions and merits, and preordaineth all things for the salvation of His elect. We must not, therefore, despair when we are tempted, but the more fervently pray to God to help us in every tribulation: Who, of a truth, according to the sayings of St. Paul, will make such issue with the temptation, that we are able to sustain it.

Let us then humble our souls under the hand of God in every temptation and tribulation, for the humble in spirit, He will save and exalt. In temptation and tribulations, it is proved what progress man has made; and there also is great merit, and virtue is made more manifest.

Now turn to page 2, For Prayers, etc.

TENTH DAY

Imitation: Book 3, Chapter 10

**That it is sweet to despise the world and to
serve God**

Now, will I speak again, O Lord, and will not be
silent, I will say in the hearing of my God and my
King Who is on high: Oh, how great is the abundance
of Thy sweetness, O Lord, which Thou hast hidden
for those that fear Thee! But what art Thou, for those
who love Thee? What, to those who serve Thee with
their whole heart? Unspeakable indeed is the sweetness of Thy contemplation, which Thou bestowest on
those who love Thee. In this most of all hast Thou
showed me the sweetness of Thy love, that when I
had no being, Thou didst make me; and when I was
straying far from Thee, Thou brought me back again,
that I might serve Thee: and Thou hast commanded
me to serve Thee. O Fountain of everlasting love,
what shall I say of Thee? How can I forget Thee, Who
hast vouchsafed to remember me even after I was cor-
rupted and lost? Beyond all hope Thou showest
mercy to Thy servant; and beyond all desert, hast
Thou manifested Thy grace and friendship. What
return shall I make to Thee for this favor? For it is
granted to all who forsake these things, to renounce
the world, and to assume the monastic life. Is it much
that I should serve Thee, Whom the whole creation is
bound to serve? It ought not to seem much to me to
serve Thee; but this does rather appear great and
wonderful to me, that Thou vouchsafest to receive
one so wretched and unworthy as Thy servant.

It is a great honor, a great glory, to serve Thee, and to despise all things for Thee, for they who willingly subject themselves to Thy holy service, shall have great grace. They shall experience the most sweet consolation of the Holy Spirit, who for the love of Thee, have cast aside all carnal delight.

Now turn to page 2, For Prayers, etc.

ELEVENTH DAY

Imitation: Book 1, Chapter 25

Of the Fervent Amendment of our whole life

When a certain anxious person, who oftentimes wavered between hope and fear, once overcome with sadness, threw himself upon the ground in prayer, before one of the altars in the Church and thinking these things in his mind, said "Oh, if I only knew how to persevere," that very instant he heard within him, this heavenly answer: "And if thou didst know this, what would thou do? Do now what you would do, and thou shall be perfectly secure." And immediately being consoled, and comforted, he committed himself to the Divine Will, and his anxious thoughts ceased. He no longer wished for curious things; searching to find out what would happen to him, but studied rather to learn what was the acceptable and perfect will of God for the beginning and the perfection of every good work.

"Hope in the Lord," said the Prophet, "And do all good, and inhabit the land, and thou shall be fed of the riches thereof." There is one thing that keeps many back from spiritual progress, and from fervor in amendment, namely: the labor that is necessary for the struggle. And assuredly they especially advance beyond others in virtues, who strive the most manfully to overcome the very things which are the hardest and most contrary to them. For there a man does profit more and merit more abundant grace, when he does most to overcome himself and mortify his spirit. All have not, indeed, equal difficulties to overcome and mortify, but a diligent and zealous person will make a greater progress though he have more passions than another, who is well regulated but less fervent in the pursuit of virtues.

Now turn to page 2, For Prayers, etc.

TWELFTH DAY

Imitation: Book 1, Chapter 25

And, whatever you see that is worthy of blame, take care that you do not do yourself, or if you have ever done so, study to amend as soon as possible. As your eye observes others, so again, you are observed by others. How pleasant and sweet it is to see brethren fervent and devout, well-mannered and well-disciplined! How sad and afflicting to see them disorderly, and not practicing the things they are called to do. How mischievous it is to neglect that purpose of their vocations, and to turn their minds to what is not their business. Be mindful of the purpose you have undertaken, and place before you the image of the Crucified. Well may you be ashamed when looking into the Life of Jesus Christ, that as yet you have not studied more to conform yourself to Him, long as you have been in the way of God.

The religious who exercises himself earnestly and devoutly in the most holy life and Passion of our Lord shall find there abundantly all that is useful and necessary for him, nor need he seek out of Jesus, for anything better. Oh, if the Crucified Jesus should come into your heart, how quickly and sufficiently learned would you be. The fervent and diligent man is ready for all things. It is harder labor to withstand our vices and passions than to toil at bodily labors. He that shuns not small defects, little by little, falls into greater ones. You will always be glad in the evening if you spent the day profitably. Watch over yourself, stir up yourself, and whatever may become of others, neglect not yourself. In proportion as you do violence to yourself, the greater progress will you make. Amen . . .

END PART I

Now turn to page 2, For Prayers, etc.

PART II

Theme: KNOWLEDGE OF SELF

rayers, examens, reflection, acts of renouncement of our own will, of contrition for our sins, of contempt of self, all performed at the feet of Mary, for it is from her that we hope for light to know ourselves. It is near her, that we shall be able to measure the abyss of our miseries without despairing. We should employ all our pious actions in asking for a knowledge of ourselves and contrition of our sins: and we should do this in a spirit of piety. During this period, we shall consider not so much the opposition that exists between the spirit of Jesus and ours, as the miserable and humiliating state to which our sins have reduced us. Moreover, the True Devotion being an easy, short, sure and perfect way to arrive at that union with our Lord, which is Christlike perfection, we shall enter seriously upon this way, strongly convinced of our misery and helplessness. But, how attain this without a knowledge of ourselves?

PRAYERS TO BE RECITED DURING THESE NEXT SEVEN DAYS
(From the 13th day to the 19th day)

Litany of the Holy Ghost
(For private devotion only)

Lord, have mercy on us.
Christ, have mercy on us.
Lord, have mercy on us.

Father, all powerful, *have mercy on us.*
Jesus, Eternal Son of the Father, Redeemer of the
       world, *save us.*
Spirit of the Father and the Son, boundless life
      of both, *sanctify us.*
Holy Trinity, *hear us.*
Holy Ghost, Who proceedest from the Father and
      the Son, *enter our hearts.*
Holy Ghost, Who are equal to the Father and the
      Son, *enter our hearts.*
Promise of God the Father,
Ray of heavenly light,
Author of all good,
Source of heavenly water,
Consuming fire,
Ardent Charity,
Spiritual unction,
Spirit of love and truth,
Spirit of wisdom and understanding,
Spirit of counsel and fortitude,
Spirit of knowledge and piety,
Spirit of the fear of the Lord,
Spirit of grace and prayer,
Spirit of peace and meekness,
Spirit of modesty and innocence,
Holy Ghost, the Comforter,
Holy Ghost, the Sanctifier,
Holy Ghost, Who governest the Church,
Gift of God, the Most High,
Spirit Who fillest the universe,
Spirit of the adoption of the children of God,
Holy Ghost, *inspire us with horror of sin.*

HAVE MERCY ON US

Holy Ghost, *come and renew the face of the earth.*
Holy Ghost, *shed Thy light in our souls.*
Holy Ghost, *engrave Thy law in our hearts.*
Holy Ghost, *inflame us with the flame of Thy Love.*
Holy Ghost, *open to us the treasures of Thy graces.*
Holy Ghost, *teach us to pray well.*
Holy Ghost, *enlighten us with Thy heavenly inspirations.*
Holy Ghost, *lead us in the way of salvation.*
Holy Ghost, *grant us the only necessary knowledge.*
Holy Ghost, *inspire in us the practice of good.*
Holy Ghost, *grant us the merits of all virtues.*
Holy Ghost, *make us persevere in justice.*
Holy Ghost, *be Thou our everlasting reward.*
Lamb of God, Who takest away the sins of the
        world, *send us Thy Holy Ghost.*
Lamb of God, Who takest away the sins of the
        world, *pour down into our souls the gifts of the
        Holy Ghost.*
Lamb of God, Who takest away the sins of the
        world, *grant us the Spirit of wisdom and piety.*
V/. Come, Holy Ghost! Fill the hearts of Thy faithful.
R/. And enkindle in them the fire of Thy Love.

Let us pray

Grant, O merciful Father, that Thy Divine Spirit enlighten, inflame and purify us, that He may penetrate us with His heavenly dew and make us fruitful in good works; through our Lord Jesus Christ, Thy Son, Who with Thee, in the unity of the Spirit, liveth and reigneth forever and ever. Amen.

Litany of the Blessed Virgin

Lord, have mercy on us.
Christ, have mercy on us.
Lord, have mercy on us.
Christ, hear us.
Christ, graciously hear us.
God the Father of heaven, have mercy on us.
God the Son, Redeemer of the world, have mercy
    on us.
God the Holy Ghost, have mercy on us.
Holy Trinity, one God, have mercy on us.
Holy Mary,
Holy Mother of God,
Holy Virgin of virgins,
Mother of Christ,
Mother of divine grace,
Mother most pure,
Mother most chaste,
Mother inviolate
Mother undefiled,
Mother most amiable,
Mother most admirable,
Mother of good counsel,
Mother of our Creator,
Mother of our Savior,
Virgin most prudent,
Virgin most venerable,
Virgin most renowned,
Virgin most powerful,
Virgin most merciful,
Virgin most faithful,

PRAY FOR US

Mirror of justice,
Seat of wisdom,
Cause of our joy,
Spiritual vessel,
Vessel of honor,
Singular vessel of devotion,
Mystical rose,
Tower of David,
Tower of ivory,
House of gold,
Ark of the covenant,
Gate of heaven,
Morning star,
Health of the sick,
Refuge of sinners,
Comforter of the afflicted,
Help of Christians,
Queen of Angels,
Queen of Patriarchs,
Queen of Prophets,
Queen of Apostles,
Queen of Martyrs,
Queen of Confessors,
Queen of Virgins,
Queen of all Saints,
Queen conceived without original sin,
Queen assumed into heaven.
Queen of the most holy Rosary,
Queen of Peace.

PRAY FOR US

Lamb of God, Who takest away the sins of the
        world., *spare us, O Lord.*
Lamb of God, Who takest away the sins of the
        world, *graciously hear us, O Lord.*

Lamb of God, Who takest away the sins of the
world, *have mercy on us.*
V/. Pray for us, O holy Mother of God.
V/. That we may be made worthy of the promises
of Christ.

Let us pray

Grant unto us, Thy servants, we beseech Thee, O
Lord God, at all times to enjoy health of soul and
body; and by the glorious intercession of Blessed
Mary, ever virgin, when freed from the sorrows of
this present life, to enter into that joy which hath no
end. Through Christ our Lord.
R/. Amen.

Ave Maris Stella

Hail, bright star of ocean,
    God's own Mother blest,
Ever sinless Virgin,
    Gate of heavenly rest.

Taking that sweet Ave
    Which from Gabriel came,
Peace confirm within us,
    Changing Eva's name.

Break the captives' fetters,
    Light on blindness pour,
All our ills expelling,
    Every bliss implore.

Show thyself a Mother;
    May the Word Divine,
Born for us thy Infant,

Hear our prayers through thine.

Virgin all excelling,
   Mildest of the mild,
Freed from guilt, preserve us,
   Pure and undefiled.

Keep our life all spotless,
   Make our way secure,
Till we find in Jesus
   Joy forevermore.

Through the highest heaven
   To the Almighty Three,
Father, Son and Spirit,
   One same Glory be. Amen.

THIRTEENTH DAY

St. Luke: Chapter 11: 1-11

The Lord's prayer

Now once he was in a certain place praying, and when he had finished one of his disciples said, "Lord, teach us to pray, just as John taught his disciples". He said to them, "Say this when you pray:
   Father, may your name be held holy,
   your kingdom come;
   give us each day our daily bread,
   and forgive us our sins,
   for we ourselves forgive each one who is in
      debt to us.

The importunate friend

He also said to them, "Suppose one of you has a friend and goes to him in the middle of the night to say, 'My friend, lend me three loaves, because a friend of mine on his travels has just arrived at my house and I have nothing to offer him' "; and the man answers from inside the house, "Do not bother me. The door is bolted now, and my children and I are in bed; I cannot get up to give it to you". I tell you, if the man does not get up and give it to him for friendship's sake, persistence will be enough to make him get up and give his friend all he wants.

Effective prayer

So I say to you: Ask, and it will be given to you; search, and you will find; knock, and the door will be opened to you. For the one who asks always receives; the one who searches always finds; the one who knocks will always have the door opened to him.

Now turn to page 21, For Prayers, etc.

FOURTEENTH DAY

Imitation: Book 3, Chapter 13

Of the obedience of a humble heart; after the example of Jesus Christ

Son, he who strives to withdraw himself from obedience, withdraws himself from grace, and he that seeks particular privileges loses such as are in

28

common, He who does not freely and willingly submit himself to his superior shows that his flesh is not as yet perfectly obedient, but instead is often rebellious. Learn then to submit yourself readily to your superior, if you desire to subdue your own flesh. For sooner is the exterior enemy overcome, if the inward man be not laid waste; there is not a more troublesome or worrisome enemy to the soul than yourself when you are not agreeing with the spirit. You must in earnest conceive a true contempt of yourself, if you will prevail against flesh and blood, because as yet, you love yourself too inordinately; therefore do you fear to resign yourself entirely to the will of others. But what great matter is this, if you who are but dust and a mere nothing, submit yourself to man for God's sake, when I the Almighty, and the Most High, Who created all things out of nothing for thy sake, humbly subjected Myself to man.

Imitation: Of the obedience of a humble heart; after the example of Jesus Christ

I became the most humble and the most abject of all men, that you might overcome your pride. Learn O dust, to obey; learn to humble yourself, and how to bow under the feet of all. Learn to break your own will, and yield yourself up to all subjection.

Now turn to page 21, For Prayers, etc.

FIFTEENTH DAY

St. Luke: Chapter 13: 1-5

Examples inviting repentance

It was just about this time that some people arrived and told him about the Galileans whose blood Pilate had mingled with that of their sacrifices. At this he said to them, "Do you suppose these Galileans who suffered like that were greater sinners than any other Galileans? They were not, I tell you. No; but unless you repent you will all perish as they did. Or those eighteen on whom the tower at Siloam fell and killed them? Do you suppose that they were more guilty than all the other people living in Jerusalem? They were not, I tell you. No; but unless you repent you will all perish as they did".

True Devotion: No. 81, 82

We need Mary in order to die to ourselves

In order to rid ourselves of self, we must die to ourselves daily. This is to say, we must renounce the operation of the powers of our soul, and the senses of our body. We must see as if we saw not, understand as if we understood not and make use of all the things of this world, as if we made no use of them at all. This is what St. Paul calls dying daily: "Unless the grain of wheat falling in the ground die, itself remaineth alone, and bringeth forth no good fruit." If we do not die to ourselves, and if the holiest devotions do not incline us to the necessary and useful death, we shall bring forth no fruit worth

30

anything, and our devotion will become useless.

We must choose, therefore, among all the devotions to the Blessed Virgin, the one which draws us most toward this death to ourselves, inasmuch as it will be the best and most sanctifying.

Now turn to page 21, For Prayers, etc.

SIXTEENTH DAY

True Devotion: No. 228

Preparatory Exercises

During the first week, we should offer up all our prayers and pious actions to ask for a knowledge of ourselves and contrition for our sins: and we should do this in a spirit of humility. For that end, we can, if we choose, meditate on our inward corruption, as explained before. We can look upon ourselves, during these days, as snails, crawling things, toads, swine, serpents, and unclean animals; or we can reflect on the three considerations of St. Bernard: the vileness of our origin, the dishonors of our present state, and our ending as food for worms. We should pray our Lord and the Holy Ghost to enlighten us, and for that we might use the ejaculation, "Lord, that I may see!" or "May I know myself" or "Come Holy Ghost," together with the Litany of the Holy Ghost. We should have recourse to the Blessed Virgin and ask her to grant this immense grace, which must be the foundation of all others, for this end, we should say daily: Ave Maris Stella, and the Litany of the Blessed Virgin.

Imitation: Book 2, Chapter 5

Of self-consideration

We may not trust too much to ourselves; for grace and understanding are often wanting in us; there is but little light and this we may soon lose by negligence. Oftentimes we are quite unconscious how blind we are. We often do amiss, and do worse in excusing ourselves. Sometimes we are moved by passion, and think it zeal. We blame little things in others and overlook great things in ourselves. We are quick enough in perceiving and weighing what we bear from others; but we think little of what others have to bear with us. He that should well and justly weigh his own doings would find little cause to judge harshly of another.

Now turn to page 21, For Prayers, etc.

SEVENTEENTH DAY

Imitation: Book 1, Chapter 24

Of judgement and punishment of sinners

In all things look to the end and how you will stand before the strict judge, from Whom there is nothing hid, Who takes no bribes, receives no excuses, but will judge that which is just. O miserable sinner, O foolish sinner, what will you answer to God, Who knows all your evil deeds. – you who are sometimes afraid of an angry man? Why don't you provide yourself against the day of judgement? When no man can be excused or defended by another, but each one will have enough to answer for himself?

St. Luke: Chapter 16: 1-8

The crafty steward

He also said to his disciples, "There was a rich man and he had a steward who was denounced to him for being wasteful with his property. He called for the man and said, 'What is this I hear about you? Draw me up an account of your stewardship because you are not to be my steward any longer.' Then the steward said to himself, 'Now that my master is taking the stewardship from me, what am I to do? Dig? I am not strong enough. Go begging? I should be too ashamed. Ah, I know what I will do to make sure that when I am dismissed from office there will be some to welcome me into their homes."

Then he called his master's debtors one by one. To the first he said, "How much do you owe my master?" "One hundred measures of oil" was the reply. The steward said, "Here, take your bond; sit down straight away and write fifty". To another he said, "And you, sir, how much do you owe?" "One hundred measures of wheat" was the reply. The steward said, "Here, take your bond and write eighty".

The master praised the dishonest steward for his astuteness. For the children of this world are more astute in dealing with their own kind than are the children of light.

Now turn to page 21, For Prayers, etc.

EIGHTEENTH DAY

St. Luke: Chapter 17: 1-10

On leading others astray

He said to his disciples, "Obstacles are sure to come, but alas for the one who provides them! It would be better for him to be thrown into the sea with a millstone put round his neck than that he should lead astray a single one of these little ones. Watch yourselves!

Brotherly correction

If your brother does something wrong, reprove him and, if he is sorry, forgive him. And if he wrongs you seven times a day and seven times comes back to you and says, "I am sorry", you must forgive him.

The power of faith

The apostles said to the Lord, "Increase our faith". The Lord replied, "Were your faith the size of a mustard seed you could say to this mulberry tree, 'Be uprooted and planted in the sea', and it would obey you."

Humble service

Which of you, with a servant ploughing or minding sheep, would say to him when he returned from the fields, "Come and have your meal immediately"? Would he not be more likely to say, "Get my supper laid; make yourself tidy and wait on me while I eat and drink. You can eat and drink your-

self afterwards"? Must he be grateful to the servant
for doing what he was told? So with you: when you
have done all you have been told to do, say, "We are
merely servants: we have done no more than our
duty".

Imitation: Book 3, Chapter 47

**That all grievous things are to be endured
for life everlasting**
    Son, let not your labors which you have under-
taken for My sake crush you, neither let tribulations,
from whatever source, cast you down, but in every
occurrence let My promise strengthen and console
you. I am sufficient in recompense to you beyond all
bounds and measures. It is not long you have to
labor here, nor will you always be oppressed with
sorrows. Wait a little while and you shall see a
speedy end of suffering.

Now turn to page 21, For Prayers, etc.

NINETEENTH DAY

St. Luke: Chapter 18: 15-30

Jesus and the children
    People even brought little children to him, for
him to touch them; but when the disciples saw this
they turned them away. But Jesus called the children
to him and said, "Let the little children come to me,
and do not stop them; for it is to such as these that
the kingdom of God belongs. I tell you solemnly,

anyone who does not welcome the kingdom of God like a little child will never enter it."

The rich aristocrat

A member of one of the leading families put this question to him, "Good Master, what have I to do to inherit eternal life?" Jesus said to him, "Why do you call me good? No one is good but God alone. You know the commandments: You must not commit adultery; You must not kill; You must not steal; You must not bring false witness; Honor your father and mother." He replied, "I have kept all these from my earliest days till now". And when Jesus heard this he said, "There is still one thing you lack. Sell all that you own and distribute the money to the poor, and you will have treasure in heaven; then come, follow me." But when he heard this he was filled with sadness, for he was very rich.

The danger of riches

Jesus looked at him and said, "How hard it is for those who have riches to make their way into the kingdom of God! Yes, it is easier for a camel to pass through the eye of a needle than for a rich man to enter the kingdom of God." "In that case," said the listeners, "Who can be saved?" "Things that are impossible for men," he replied, "are possible for God."

The reward of renunciation

Then Peter said, "What about us? We left all we had to follow you." He said to them, "I tell you solemnly, there is no one who has left house, wife, brothers, parents or children for the sake of the kingdom of God who will not be given repayment many times over in this present time and, in the world to come, eternal life."

Now turn to page 21, For Prayers, etc.

PART III

Theme: KNOWLEDGE OF MARY

cts of love, pious affections for the Blessed Virgin, imitation of her virtues, especially her profound humility, her lively faith, her blind obedience, her continual mental prayer, her mortification in all things, her surpassing purity, her ardent charity, her heroic patience, her angelic sweetness and her divine wisdom: "these being," as St. Louis De Montfort says, "the ten principal virtues of the Blessed Virgin."

We must unite ourselves to Jesus through Mary – this is the characteristic of our devotion; therefore Saint Louis De Montfort asks that we employ ourselves in acquiring a knowledge of the Blessed Virgin. Mary is our sovereign and our mediatrix, our Mother and our Mistress. Let us then endeavor to know the effects of this royalty, of this mediation, and of this maternity, as well as the grandeurs and prerogatives which are the foundation or consequences thereof. Our blessed Mother is also perfect - a mold wherein we are able to be molded in order to make her intentions and dispositions ours. This we cannot achieve without studying the interior life of Mary, namely, her virtues, her sentiments, her actions, her participation in the mysteries of Christ and her union with Him.

PRAYERS TO BE RECITED DURING THESE NEXT SEVEN DAYS

Litany of the Holy Ghost
(For private devotion only)

Lord, have mercy on us.

Christ, have mercy on us.

Lord, have mercy on us.

Father, all powerful, *have mercy on us.*

Jesus, Eternal Son of the Father, Redeemer of the world, *save us.*

Spirit of the Father and the Son, boundless life of both, *sanctify us.*

Holy Trinity, *hear us.*

Holy Ghost, Who proceedest from the Father and the Son, *enter our hearts.*

Holy Ghost, Who are equal to the Father and the Son, *enter our hearts.*

Promise of God the Father,

Ray of heavenly light,

Author of all good,

Source of heavenly water,

Consuming fire,

Ardent Charity,

Spiritual unction,

Spirit of love and truth,

HAVE MERCY ON US

38

Spirit of wisdom and understanding,
Spirit of counsel and fortitude,
Spirit of knowledge and piety,
Spirit of the fear of the Lord,
Spirit of grace and prayer,
Spirit of peace and meekness,
Spirit of modesty and innocence,
Holy Ghost, the Comforter,
Holy Ghost, the Sanctifier,
Holy Ghost, Who governest the Church,
Gift of God, the Most High,
Spirit Who fillest the universe,

HAVE MERCY ON US

Spirit of the adoption of the children of God,
Holy Ghost, *inspire us with horror of sin.*
Holy Ghost, *come and renew the face of the earth.*
Holy Ghost, *shed Thy light in our souls.*
Holy Ghost, *engrave Thy law in our hearts.*
Holy Ghost, *inflame us with the fire of Thy Love.*
Holy Ghost, *open to us the treasures of Thy graces.*
Holy Ghost, *teach us to pray well.*
Holy Ghost, *enlighten us with Thy heavenly inspirations.*
Holy Ghost, *lead us in the way of salvation.*
Holy Ghost, *grant us the only necessary knowledge.*
Holy Ghost, *inspire in us the practice of good.*
Holy Ghost, *grant us the merits of all virtues.*
Holy Ghost, *make us persevere in justice.*
Holy Ghost, *be Thou our everlasting reward.*
Lamb of God, Who takest away the sins of the
world, *send us Thy Holy Ghost.*
Lamb of God, Who takest away the sins of the
world, *pour down into our souls the gifts of the
Holy Ghost.*

Lamb of God, Who takest away the sins of the
      world, *grant us the Spirit of wisdom and piety.*
V/. Come, Holy Ghost! Fill the hearts of Thy faithful.
V/. And enkindle in them the fire of Thy Love.

Let us pray

Grant, O merciful Father, that Thy Divine Spirit
enlighten, inflame and purify us, that He may penetrate us with His heavenly dew and make us fruitful in good works; through our Lord Jesus Christ,
Thy Son, Who with Thee, in the unity of the Spirit,
liveth and reigneth forever and ever. Amen.

Litany of the Blessed Virgin

Lord, have mercy on us.
Christ, have mercy on us.
Lord, have mercy on us.
Christ, hear us.
Christ, graciously hear us.
God the Father of heaven, have mercy on us.
God the Son, Redeemer of the world, have mercy
      on us.
God the Holy Ghost, have mercy on us.
Holy Trinity, one God, have mercy on us.
Holy Mary, .
Holy Mother of God,
Holy Virgin of virgins,
Mother of Christ,
Mother of divine grace,
Mother most pure,
Mother most chaste,

PRAY FOR US

40

Mother inviolate
Mother undefiled,
Mother most amiable,
Mother most admirable,
Mother of good counsel,
Mother of our Creator,
Mother of our Savior,
Virgin most prudent,
Virgin most venerable,
Virgin most renowned,
Virgin most powerful,
Virgin most merciful,
Virgin most faithful,
Mirror of justice,
Seat of wisdom,
Cause of our joy,
Spiritual vessel,
Vessel of honor,
Singular vessel of devotion,
Mystical rose,
Tower of David,
Tower of ivory,
House of gold,
Ark of the covenant,
Gate of heaven,
Morning star,
Health of the sick,
Refuge of sinners,
Comforter of the afflicted,
Help of Christians,
Queen of Angels,
Queen of Patriarchs,

PRAY FOR US

Queen of Prophets,
Queen of Apostles,
Queen of Martyrs,
Queen of Confessors,
Queen of Virgins,
Queen of all Saints,
Queen conceived without original sin,
Queen assumed into heaven.
Queen of the most holy Rosary,
Queen of Peace.

Lamb of God, Who takest away the sins of the
    world., *spare us, O Lord.*

Lamb of God, Who takest away the sins of the
    world, *graciously hear us, O Lord.*

Lamb of God, Who takest away the sins of the
    world, *have mercy on us.*

V/. Pray for us, O holy Mother of God.

V/. That we may be made worthy of the promises
    of Christ.

Let us pray

Grant unto us, Thy servants, we beseech Thee, O
Lord God, at all times to enjoy health of soul and
body; and by the glorious intercession of Blessed
Mary, ever virgin, when freed from the sorrows of
this present life, to enter into that joy which hath no
end. Through Christ our Lord.
R/. Amen.

Ave Maris Stella

Hail, bright star of ocean,
God's own Mother blest,
Ever sinless Virgin,
Gate of heavenly rest.

Taking that sweet Ave
Which from Gabriel came,
Peace confirm within us,
Changing Eva's name.

Break the captives' fetters,
Light on blindness pour,
All our ills expelling,
Every bliss implore.

Show thyself a Mother;
May the Word Divine,
Born for us thy Infant,
Hear our prayers through thine.

Virgin all excelling,
Mildest of the mild,
Freed from guilt, preserve us,
Pure and undefiled.

Keep our life all spotless,
Make our way secure,
Till we find in Jesus
Joy forevermore.

Through the highest heaven
To the Almighty Three,
Father, Son and Spirit,
One same Glory be. Amen.

St. Louis De Montfort's Prayer to Mary

Hail Mary, beloved Daughter of the Eternal Father. Hail Mary, admirable Mother of the Son. Hail Mary, faithful Spouse of the Holy Ghost. Hail Mary, my Mother, my loving Mistress, my powerful sovereign. Hail, my joy, my glory, my heart and my soul. Thou art all mine by mercy, and I am thine by justice. But I am not yet sufficiently thine. I now give myself wholly to thee without keeping anything back for myself or others. If thou seest anything in me which does not belong to thee, I beseech thee to take it and make thyself the absolute Mistress of all that is mine.

Destroy in me all that may displease God; root it up and bring it to nought. Place and cultivate in me everything that is pleasing to thee. May the light of thy faith dispel the darkness of my mind. May thy profound humility take the place of my pride; may thy sublime contemplation check the distractions of my wandering imagination. May the continuous sight of God fill my memory with His presence; may the burning love of thy heart inflame the lukewarmness of mine. May thy virtues take the place of my sins; may thy merits be my only adornment in the sight of God and make up for all that is wanting in me. Finally, dearly beloved Mother, grant, if it be possible, that I may have no other spirit but thine to know Jesus, and His Divine Will; that I may have no other soul but thine to praise and glorify God; that I may have no other heart but thine to love God with a love as pure and ardent as thine.

I do not ask thee for visions, revelations, sensible devotions, or spiritual pleasures. It is thy privilege to see God clearly, it is thy privilege to enjoy heavenly bliss; it is thy privilege to triumph gloriously in heaven at the right hand of thy Son and to hold absolute sway over angels, men and demons.

It is thy privilege to dispose of all the gifts of God, just as thou willest. Such, O heavenly Mary, the 'best part', which the Lord has given thee, and which shall never be taken away from thee - and this thought fills my heart with joy. As for my part here below, I wish for no other than that which was thine, to believe sincerely without spiritual pleasures, to suffer joyfully without human consolation, to die continually to myself without respite, and to work zealously and unselfishly for thee until death, as the humblest of thy servants. The only grace I beg thee, for me, is that every moment of the day, and every moment of my life, I may say "Amen, so be it, to all that thou art doing in heaven. Amen, so be it, to all thou didst do while on earth. Amen, so be it, to all thou art doing in my soul," so that thou alone mayest fully glorify Jesus in me for time and eternity. Amen.

Recitation of the Rosary . . .

45

TWENTIETH DAY

St. Luke: Chapter 2, 16-21; 42-52

So they hurried away and found Mary and Joseph, and the baby lying in the manger. When they saw the child they repeated what they had been told about him, and everyone who heard it was astonished at what the shepherds had to say. As for Mary, she treasured all these things and pondered them in her heart. And the shepherds went back glorifying and praising God for all they had heard and seen; it was exactly as they had been told.

The circumcision of Jesus

When the eighth day came and the child was to be circumcised, they gave him the name Jesus, the name the angel had given him before his conception.

****

When he was twelve years old, they went up for the feast as usual. When they were on their way home after the feast, the boy Jesus stayed behind in Jerusalem without his parents knowing it. They assumed he was with the caravan, and it was only after a day's journey that they went to look for him among their relations and acquaintances. When they failed to find him they went back to Jerusalem looking for him everywhere.

Three days later, they found him in the Temple sitting among the doctors, listening to them, and asking them questions; and all those who heard him were astounded at his intelligence and his replies. They were overcome when they saw him, and his mother said to him, "My child, why have you done this to us? See how worried your father and I have been, looking for you." "Why were you looking for me?" he replied "Did you not know that I must be busy with my Father's affairs?" But they did not understand what he meant.

The hidden life at Nazareth resumed

He then went down with them and came to Nazareth and lived under their authority. His mother stored up all these things in her heart. And Jesus increased in wisdom, in stature, and in favor with God and men.

Now turn to page 38, For Prayers, etc.

TWENTY-FIRST DAY

Secret of Mary: Nos. 23-24

True Devotion to Our Blessed Lady

If we would go up to God, and be united with Him, we must use the same means He used to come down to us to be made Man and to impart His graces to us. This means is a true devotion to our Blessed Lady. There are several true devotions to our Lady: here I do not speak of those which are false.

The first consists in fulfilling our Christian duties, avoiding mortal sin, acting more out of love than with fear, praying to our Lady now and then, honoring her as the Mother of God, yet without having any special devotion to her.

The second consists in entertaining for our Lady more perfect feelings of esteem and love, of confidence and veneration. It leads us to join the Confraternities of the Holy Rosary and of the Scapular, to recite the five or the fifteen decades of the Holy Rosary, to honor Mary's images and altars, to publish her praises and to enroll ourselves in her sodalities. This devotion is good, holy and praiseworthy if we keep ourselves free from sin. But it is not so perfect as the next, nor so efficient in severing our soul from creatures, in detaching ourselves in order to be united with Jesus Christ.

The third devotion to our Lady, known and practiced by very few persons, is this I am about to disclose to you, predestinate soul. It consists in giving one's self entirely and as a slave to Mary, and to Jesus through Mary, and after that, to do all that we do, through Mary, with Mary, in Mary and for Mary. We should choose a special feast day on which we give, consecrate and sacrifice to Mary, voluntarily, lovingly and without constraint, entirely and without reserve: our body and soul, our exterior property, such as house, family and income, and also our interior and spiritual possessions: namely, our merits, graces, virtues, and satisfactions.

Now turn to page 38, For Prayers, etc.

TWENTY-SECOND DAY

True Devotion: Nos. 105-110.

The characteristics of true devotion

Interior: True devotion to our Lady is interior: that is, it comes from the mind and the heart, it flows from the esteem we have for her, the high idea we have formed of her greatness and the love which we have for her.

Tender: It is tender, that is, full of confidence in her like a child's confidence in his loving mother. This confidence makes the soul have recourse to her in all its bodily and mental necessities, with much simplicity, trust and tenderness.

Holy: This devotion to our Lady is holy: that is to say, it leads the soul to avoid sin and imitate the virtues of the Blessed Virgin, particularly her profound humility, her lively faith, her blind obedience, her continual prayer, her universal mortification, her divine purity, her ardent charity, her heroic patience, her angelic sweetness and her divine wisdom. These are the ten principal virtues of the most holy Virgin.

Constant: It is constant, that is to say, it confirms the soul in good, and does not let it easily abandon its spiritual exercises. It makes it courageous in opposing the world and its fashions and maxims; the flesh in its weariness and passions; and the devil in his temptations, so that a person truly devout to our Blessed Lady is neither changeable, irritable, scrupulous or timid.

Disinterested: True devotion to our Lady is disinterested: that is to say, it inspires the soul, not to seek itself but God only, and God in His holy Mother. A true client of Mary does not serve that august Queen from a spirit of lucre and interest, nor for his own good, whether temporal or eternal, corporal or spiritual, but exclusively because she deserves to be served and God alone in her.

Now turn to page 38, For Prayers, etc.

TWENTY-THIRD DAY

True Devotion: Nos. 120-121

Nature of perfect devotion to the Blessed Virgin or perfect consecration to Jesus Christ

All our perfection consists in being conformed, united and consecrated to Jesus Christ; and therefore the most perfect of all devotions is, without any doubt, that which the most perfectly conforms, unites and consecrates us to Jesus Christ. Now Mary, being the most conformed of all creatures to Jesus Christ, it follows that of all devotions, that which most consecrates and conforms the soul to our Lord is devotion to His holy Mother; that the more a soul is consecrated to Mary, the more it is consecrated to Jesus Christ (Sec. 120). Hence it comes to pass that the most perfect consecration to Jesus Christ is nothing else but a perfect consecration, of ourselves, to the Blessed Virgin, and this is the devotion which I teach; or, in other words, a perfect renewal of the vows and promises of Holy Baptism. This devotion, consists then, in giving ourselves entirely to our

Lady, in order to belong entirely to Jesus Christ, through her.

We must give her: our body, with all its senses and members; our soul with all its powers; our exterior goods of fortune, whether present or to come; our interior and spiritual goods, which are our merits, our virtues and our good works, past, present, and future. In a word, we must give her all we have in the order of nature and in the order of grace and all that may become ours in the future in the orders of nature, grace and glory; and this we must do without reserve of so much as one farthing, one hair, or one least good intention. We must do it also for eternity, and we must do it without pretending to, or hoping for any other recompense for our offering and service, except the honor of belonging to Jesus Christ, through Mary and in Mary even though that sweet Mistress were not, as she always is, the most generous and the most grateful of creatures.

Now turn to page 38, For Prayers, etc.

TWENTY-FOURTH DAY

True Devotion: Nos. 152-164

This devotion is an easy, short, perfect and secure way of attaining union with our Lord, in which union the perfection of a Christian consists. *It is an easy way:* It is the way which Jesus Christ Himself trod in coming to us in which there is no obstacle in reaching Him. It is true that we can attain divine union by other roads, but it is by many crosses and strange deaths, and with many more difficulties which we shall find it hard to overcome.

It is a short way: This devotion to our Blessed Lady is a short road to find Jesus Christ, both because it is a road from which we do not stray, and because as I have just said, it is a road which we tread with joy and facility, and consequently with promptitude. We make more progress in a brief period of submission to and dependence on Mary, than in whole years of following our own will and of relying upon ourselves. *It is a perfect way:* This practice of devotion to our Blessed Lady is also a perfect path by which to go and unite ourselves to Jesus, because the blessed Mary is the most perfect and the most holy of creatures, and because Jesus, Who has come to us most perfectly, took no other road for His great and admirable journey. The Most High, the Incomprehensible, the Inaccessible, He Who is, had willed to come to us, little worms of earth, who are nothing. How has He done this? The Most High has come down to us perfectly and divinely, by the humble Mary, without losing anything of His Divinity and Sanctity. So it is by Mary that the very little ones are to ascend perfectly and divinely, without any fear, to the Most High. *It is a secure way:* This devotion to our Blessed Lady, is also a secure way to go to Jesus and to acquire perfection, by uniting ourselves to Him. It is a secure way because the practice which I am teaching is not new. Indeed, we cannot see how it could be condemned without overturning the foundations of Christianity. It is clear then, that this devotion is not new, and that if it is not common, that is because it is too precious to be relished and practiced by everyone. This devotion is a secure means of going to Jesus Christ, because it is the very characteristic of Our Blessed Lady to conduct us surely to Jesus.

Now turn to page 38, For Prayers, etc.

TWENTY-FIFTH DAY

True Devotion: Nos. 213-225

Wonderful Effects of This Devotion

My dear brother, be sure that if you are faithful to the interior and exterior practices of this devotion which I will point out – the following effects will take place in your soul.

First Effect: By the light which the Holy Ghost will give you through His dear Spouse, Mary, you will understand your own evil, your corruption and your incapacity for anything good. In other words, the humble Mary will communicate to you a portion of her profound humility, which will make you despise yourself, despise nobody else, but love to be despised yourself.

Second Effect: Our Blessed Lady also will give you a portion of her faith, which was the greatest of all faiths, that were ever on this earth, greater than all the faiths of all the patriarchs prophets, apostles and saints put together.

Third Effect: This Mother of fair love, will take away from your heart, all scruple and all disorder of servile fear.

Fourth Effect: Our Blessed Lady will fill you with great confidence in God and in herself because you will not be approaching Jesus by yourself, but always by that good Mother.

Fifth Effect: The soul of our Blessed Lady will communicate itself to you, to glorify the Lord. Her spirit will enter into the place of yours, to rejoice in God, her salvation, provided only that you are faithful to the practices of this devotion.

Sixth Effect: If Mary, who is the tree of life, is well cultivated in our soul by fidelity to the practices of this devotion, she will bear fruit in her own time, and her fruit is none other than Jesus Christ.

Seventh Effect: By this practice, faithfully observed, you will give Jesus more glory in a month, than by any other practice, however difficult, in many years.

Now turn to page 38, For Prayers, etc.

TWENTY-SIXTH DAY

True Devotion: Nos. 12-38

If you wish to comprehend the Mother, says a saint, comprehend the Son, for she is the worthy Mother of God. Here, let every tongue be mute. Up to this time, the divine Mary has been unknown, and that is the reason Jesus Christ is not known as He ought to be. If then the knowledge and the kingdom of Jesus Christ are to come into the world, they will be but a necessary consequence of the knowledge and the kingdom of the most holy Virgin Mary, who brought Him into the world for the first time, and will make His second advent full of splendor.

Mary, being a mere creature that has come from the hands of the Most High, is in comparison with his infinite Majesty less than an atom; or rather she is nothing at all, because He is "He Who Is," consequently that grand Lord, always independent and sufficient to Himself, never had, and has not now an absolute need of the Holy Virgin for the accomplishment of His Will, and for the manifestation of His Glory. He has but to will in order to do everything. Nevertheless, God, having willed to commence and to complete His greatest works by the Most Holy Virgin, ever since He created her, we may well think He will not change His conduct in the eternal ages; for He is God, and He changes not, either in His sentiments or in His conduct.

Mary is the queen of heaven and earth by grace, as Jesus is the King of them by nature and by conquest. Now, as the kingdom of Jesus Christ consists principally in the heart or the interior of man — according to the words, "The Kingdom of God is within you" — in like manner the kingdom of our Blessed Lady is principally in the interior of man; that is to say, his soul. And it is principally in souls that she is more glorified with her Son than in all visible creatures, and so we can call her, as the saints do, the Queen of All Hearts.

Now turn to page 38, For Prayers, etc.

PART IV

Theme:
KNOWLEDGE OF JESUS CHRIST

True Devotion: Nos. 60-67, 183, 212,
226-265

Acts of love of God, thanksgiving for the blessings of Jesus, contrition and resolution

uring this period we shall apply ourselves to the study of Jesus Christ. What is to be studied in Jesus Christ?

First: The Man-God, His grace and glory; then His rights to sovereign dominion over us; since, having renounced Satan and the world, we have taken Jesus Christ as our Lord.

Second: His interior life, namely, the virtues and the acts of His Sacred Heart; His association with Mary in the mysteries of the Annunciation and Incarnation; during His infancy and hidden life at the feast of Cana and on Calvary . . .

PRAYERS TO BE RECITED DURING THESE NEXT SEVEN DAYS

Litany of the Holy Ghost
(For private devotion only)

Lord, have mercy on us.
Christ, have mercy on us.
Lord, have mercy on us.
Father, all powerful, have mercy on us.
Jesus, Eternal Son of the Father, Redeemer of the

world, save us.

Spirit of the Father and the Son, boundless life
      of both, sanctify us.

Holy Trinity, hear us.

Holy Ghost, Who proceedest from the Father and
      the Son, enter our hearts.

Holy Ghost, Who are equal to the Father and the
      Son, enter our hearts.

Promise of God the Father,

Ray of heavenly light,

Author of all good,

Source of heavenly water,

Consuming fire,

Ardent Charity,

Spiritual unction,

Spirit of love and truth,

Spirit of wisdom and understanding,

Spirit of counsel and fortitude,

Spirit of knowledge and piety,

Spirit of the fear of the Lord,

Spirit of grace and prayer,

Spirit of peace and meekness,

Spirit of modesty and innocence,

Holy Ghost, the Comforter,

Holy Ghost, the Sanctifier,

Holy Ghost, Who governest the Church,

Gift of God, the Most High,

Spirit Who fillest the universe,

Spirit of the adoption of the children of God,

Holy Ghost, *inspire us with horror of sin.*

Holy Ghost, *come and renew the face of the earth.*

Holy Ghost, *shed Thy light in our souls.*

HAVE MERCY ON US

Holy Ghost, *engrave Thy law in our hearts.*
Holy Ghost, *inflame us with the fire of Thy Love.*
Holy Ghost, *open to us the treasures of Thy graces.*
Holy Ghost, *teach us to pray well.*
Holy Ghost, *enlighten us with Thy heavenly inspirations.*
Holy Ghost, *lead us in the way of salvation.*
Holy Ghost, *grant us the only necessary knowledge.*
Holy Ghost, *inspire in us the practice of good.*
Holy Ghost, *grant us the merits of all virtues.*
Holy Ghost, *make us persevere in justice.*
Holy Ghost, *be Thou our everlasting reward.*
Lamb of God, Who takest away the sins of the
       world, *send us Thy Holy Ghost.*
Lamb of God, Who takest away the sins of the
       world, *pour down into our souls the gifts of the*
       Holy Ghost.
Lamb of God, Who takest away the sins of the
       world, *grant us the Spirit of wisdom and piety.*
V/. Come, Holy Ghost! Fill the hearts of Thy faithful.
V/. And enkindle in them the fire of Thy Love.

Let us pray

Grant, O merciful Father, that Thy Divine Spirit enlighten, inflame and purify us, that He may penetrate us with His heavenly dew and make us fruitful in good works; through our Lord Jesus Christ, Thy Son, Who with Thee, in the unity of the Spirit, liveth and reigneth forever and ever. Amen.

Ave Maris Stella

Hail, bright star of ocean,
God's own Mother blest,
Ever sinless Virgin,
Gate of heavenly rest.

Taking that sweet Ave
Which from Gabriel came,
Peace confirm within us,
Changing Eva's name.

Break the captives' fetters,
Light on blindness pour,
All our ills expelling,
Every bliss implore.

Show thyself a Mother;
May the Word Divine,
Born for us thy Infant,
Hear our prayers through thine.

Virgin all excelling,
Mildest of the mild,
Freed from guilt, preserve us,
Pure and undefiled.

Keep our life all spotless,
Make our way secure,
Till we find in Jesus
Joy forevermore.

Through the highest heaven
    To the Almighty Three,
Father, Son and Spirit,
    One Same Glory be. Amen.

Litany of the Holy Name of Jesus

Lord, have mercy on us.
Christ, have mercy on us.
Lord, have mercy on us.
Jesus, hear us.
Jesus, graciously hear us.
God the Father of heaven,
God the Son, Redeemer of the world,
God the Holy Ghost,
Holy Trinity, one God,
Jesus, Son of the living God,
Jesus, splendor of the Father,
Jesus, brightness of eternal light,
Jesus, King of glory,
Jesus, sun of justice,
Jesus, Son of the Virgin Mary,
Jesus, most amiable,
Jesus, most admirable,
Jesus, mighty God,
Jesus, Father of the world to come,
Jesus, angel of the great counsel,
Jesus, most powerful,
Jesus, most patient,
Jesus, most obedient,
Jesus, meek and humble of heart,
Jesus, lover of chastity,
Jesus, our lover,
Jesus, God of peace,
Jesus, author of life,
Jesus, model of virtues,
Jesus, zealous for souls,

HAVE MERCY ON US

60

Jesus, our God,
Jesus, our refuge,
Jesus, Father of the poor,
Jesus, treasure of the faithful,
Jesus, Good Shepherd,
Jesus, true light,
Jesus, eternal Wisdom,
Jesus, infinite Goodness,
Jesus, our way and our life,
Jesus, joy of The Angels,
Jesus, King of Patriarchs,
Jesus, master of Apostles,
Jesus, teacher of Evangelists,
Jesus, strength of Martyrs,
Jesus, light of Confessors,
Jesus, purity of Virgins,
Jesus, Crown of all Saints,

HAVE MERCY ON US

Be merciful, *spare us, O Jesus.*
Be merciful, *graciously hear us, O Jesus.*
From all evil,
From all sin,
From Thy wrath,
From the snares of the devil,
From the spirit of fornication,
From everlasting death,
From the neglect of Thine inspirations,
Through the mystery of Thy holy Incarnation,
Through Thy nativity,
Through Thy infancy,
Through Thy most divine life,
Through Thy labors,
Through Thine agony and Passion,

JESUS, DELIVER US

Through Thy cross and dereliction,
Through Thy sufferings,
Through Thy death and burial,
Through Thy Resurrection,
Through Thine Ascension,
Through Thine institution of the most Holy
    Eucharist,
Through Thy joys,
Through Thy glory,
Lamb of God, Who takest away the sins of the
    world, *spare us, O Jesus.*
Lamb of God, Who takest away the sins of the
    world, *graciously hear us, O Jesus.*
Lamb of God, Who takest away the sins of the
    world, *have mercy on us, O Jesus.*
Jesus, hear us.
Jesus, graciously hear us.

JESUS, DELIVER US

Let us pray

O Lord Jesus Christ, Who hast said: Ask and ye shall receive; seek and ye shall find; knock and it shall be opened unto you; grant, we beseech Thee, to us who ask the gift of Thy divine love, that we may ever love Thee with all our hearts, and in all our words and actions, and never cease praising Thee.

Give us, O Lord, a perpetual love of Thy holy Name; for Thou never failest to govern those whom thou dost solidly establish in Thy love. Who livest and reignest world without end. Amen.

St. Louis De Montfort's Prayer to Jesus

O most loving Jesus, deign to let me pour forth my gratitude before Thee, for the grace Thou hast bestowed upon me in giving me to Thy holy Mother through the devotion of Holy slavery, that she may be my advocate in the presence of Thy majesty and my support in my extreme misery. Alas, O Lord! I am so wretched that without this dear Mother I should be certainly lost. Yes, Mary is necessary for me at Thy side and everywhere: that she may appease Thy just wrath, because I have so often offended Thee; that she may save me from the eternal punishment of Thy justice, which I deserve; that she may contemplate Thee, speak to Thee, pray to Thee, approach Thee and please Thee; that she may help me to save my soul and the souls of others; in short, Mary is necessary for me that I may always do Thy holy will and seek Thy greater glory in all things. Ah, would that I could proclaim throughout the whole world the mercy that Thou hast shown to me! Would that everyone might know I should be already damned, were it not for Mary! Would that I might offer worthy thanksgiving for so great a blessing! Mary is in me. Oh, what a treasure! Oh, what a consolation! And shall I not be entirely hers? Oh, what ingratitude! My dear Savior, send me death rather than such a calamity, for I would rather die than live without belonging entirely to Mary.

With St. John the Evangelist at the foot of the cross, I have taken her a thousand times for my own and as many times have given myself to her; but if

I have not yet done it as Thou, dear Jesus, dost wish, I now renew this offering as Thou desire me to renew it. And if Thou seest in my soul or my body anything that does not belong to this august princess, I pray Thee to take it and cast it far from me, for whatever in me does not belong to Mary is unworthy of Thee.

O Holy Spirit, grant me all these graces. Plant in my soul the Tree of true Life, which is Mary; cultivate it and tend it so that it may grow and blossom and bring forth the fruit of life in abundance. O Holy Spirit, give me great devotion to Mary, Thy faithful spouse; give me great confidence in her maternal heart and an abiding refuge in her mercy, so that by her Thou mayest truly form in me Jesus Christ, great and mighty, unto the fullness of His perfect age. Amen.

O, Jesus Living in Mary

O Jesus living in Mary
Come and live in Thy servants,
In the spirit of Thy holiness,
In the fullness of Thy might,
In the truth of Thy virtues,
In the perfection of Thy ways,
In the communion of Thy mysteries,
Subdue every hostile power
In Thy spirit, for the glory of the Father. Amen.

TWENTY-SEVENTH DAY

True Devotion: Nos. 61, 62

Christ our Last End

Jesus Christ our Savior, true God and true Man, ought to be the last end of all our devotions, else they are false and delusive. Jesus Christ is the Alpha and the Omega, the beginning and the end, of all things. We labor not, as the Apostle says, except to render every man perfect in Jesus Christ; because it is in Him alone that the whole plenitude of the Divinity dwells together with all the other plenitudes of graces, virtues and perfections. It is in Him alone that we have been blessed with all spiritual benediction; and He is our only Master, Who has to teach us; our only Lord on Whom we ought to depend; our only Head to Whom we must be united; our only Model to Whom we should conform ourselves; our only Physician Who can heal us; our only Shepherd Who can feed us; our only Way Who can lead us; our only Truth Whom we must believe; our only Life Who can animate us; and our only All in all things Who can satisfy us. There has been no other name given under heaven, except the name of Jesus, by which we can be saved. God has laid no other foundation of our salvation, our perfection or our glory, than Jesus Christ. Every building which is not built on that firm rock is founded upon the moving sand, and sooner or later infallibly will fall.

By Jesus Christ, with Jesus Christ, in Jesus Christ, we can do all things; we can render all honor and glory to the Father in the unity of the Holy Ghost; we can become perfect ourselves, and be to our neighbor a good odor of eternal life.

If, then, we establish solid devotion to our Blessed Lady, it is only to establish more perfectly devotion to Jesus Christ, and to provide an easy and secure means for finding Jesus Christ. Devotion to our Lady is necessary for us, as I have already shown, and will show still further hereafter, as a means of finding Jesus Christ perfectly, of loving Him tenderly, of serving Him faithfully.

Now turn to page 56, For Prayers, etc.

TWENTY-EIGHTH DAY

St. Matthew: Chapter 26: 1; 26-29; 36-46

The conspiracy against Jesus

Jesus had now finished all he wanted to say, and he told his disciples, "It will be Passover, as you know, in two days' time, and the Son of Man will be handed over to be crucified".

* * * *

The institution of the Eucharist

Now as they were eating, Jesus took some bread, and when he had said the blessing he broke it and gave it to the disciples. "Take it and eat;" he said, "this is my body." Then he took a cup, and when he had returned thanks, he gave it to them. "Drink all of you from this," he said "for this is my blood, the blood of the covenant, which is to be poured out for many for the forgiveness of sins. From now on, I tell you, I shall not drink wine until the day I drink the new wine with you in the kingdom of my Father."

* * * *

Gethsemane

Then Jesus came with them to a small estate called Gethsemane; and he said to his disciples, "Stay here while I go over there to pray". He took Peter and the two sons of Zebedee with him. And sadness came over him, and great distress. Then he said to them, "My soul is sorrowful to the point of death. Wait here and keep awake with me." And going on a little further he fell on his face and prayed. "My Father," he said, "if it is possible, let this cup pass me by. Nevertheless, let it be as you, not I, would have it." He came back to the disciples and found them sleeping, and he said to Peter, "So you had not the strength to keep awake with me one hour? You should be awake, and praying not to be put to the test. The spirit is willing, but the flesh is weak." Again, a second time, he went away and prayed: "My Father," he said, "if this cup cannot pass by without my drinking it, your will be done!" And he came again back and found them sleeping, their eyes were so heavy. Leaving them there, he went away again and prayed for the third time, "You can sleep on now and take your rest. Now the hour has come when the Son of Man is to be betrayed into the hands of sinners. Get up! Let us go! My betrayer is already close at hand."

Now turn to page 56, For Prayers, etc.

TWENTY-NINTH DAY

Imitation: Book 1, Chapter 1

Of the imitation of Christ and indifference to earthly vanities

He who follows Me does not walk in darkness. (John 8:12). Christ reminds you with these words that you must imitate His life, if you wish to be truly enlightened and freed from all blindness of heart. Your main task, therefore, should be to study the life of Our Lord.

The teaching of Christ is greater than the advice of all the saints taken together. And if you study it with His frame of mind and heart, you will find in his teaching a hidden source of consolation and strength. Unfortunately, however, so many people care little or nothing about the Word of God, even though they have heard it time and time again, because they do not have the spirit of Christ. Yet, if you really want to understand the Words of Christ, you must try to pattern your whole life on His.

What good is it to be able to explain the doctrine of the Blessed Trinity if you displease the Blessed Trinity by your lack of humility? It is a good life that makes you pleasing to God, not high-sounding words and clever expressions. It is better to feel contrition for your sins than to know how to define it. What good is it to know the entire Bible by heart and to learn the sayings of all the philosophers if you live without grace and the Love of God?

Vanity of vanities, and all is vanity, unless you

serve God and love Him with your whole heart. (Eccles. 1:2). The greatest wisdom of all is to seek the kingdom of heaven by despising the things of this world.

Now turn to page 56, For Prayers, etc.

THIRTIETH DAY

St. Matthew: Chapter 27: 36-44

The crucifixion

. . . .and then sat down and stayed there keeping guard over him.

Above his head was placed the charge against him; it read: "This is Jesus, the King of the Jews". At the same time two robbers were crucified with him, one on the right and one on the left.

The crucified Christ is mocked

The passers-by jeered at him; they shook their heads and said, "So you would destroy the Temple and rebuild it in three days! Then save yourself! If you are God's son, come down from the cross!" The chief priests with the scribes and elders mocked him in the same way. "He saved others;" they said, "he cannot save himself. He is the king of Israel; let him come down from the cross now, and we will believe in him. He puts his trust in God; now let God rescue him if he wants him. For he did say, "I am the son of God". Even the robbers who were crucified with him taunted him in the same way.

Imitation: Book 2, Chapter 12

Of the Royal Road of the Cross

To many the saying, "Deny yourself, take up your cross and follow Me," seems hard. How much harder, however, will the words on the Day of Judgement be: Depart from Me, you accursed ones, into the everlasting fire. (Matt. 25:41). Those who follow the cross willingly now, will not fear the last judgement. When the Lord comes to judge, the Sign of the Cross will be in the heavens; then will those servants of the cross, who in their life-time made themselves one with the Crucified, draw near with great trust to Christ, the judge.

Why are you afraid, then, to take up the cross when through it you can win an eternal kingdom? In the cross is salvation; in it is life; in it is protection from your enemies; in it is heavenly sweetness; in it is strength of mind; in it is joy of spirit; in it is the highest virtue; in the cross is perfect holiness.

Take up your cross and follow Jesus, and you will merit eternal life.

Now turn to page 56, For Prayers, etc.

THIRTY-FIRST DAY

Imitation: Book 4, Chapter 2

Of the Love God Shows You In The Blessed Sacrament

Trusting in Your great goodness and mercy, Lord, I come as one sick to the Physician, as one thirsty to the Fountain of Life, as one in need to the King of heaven; I come as a servant to my Master, as a creature to my Creator, as a dejected soul to my loving Comforter.

But why should You come to me? Who am I that You should give Yourself to me? How can a sinner dare show his face in Your presence? And why do You condescend to visit a sinner: You know Your servant; You know he has no good in him, and, therefore, You have no reason to grant him this great grace. Thus I confess my unworthiness; and I acknowledge Your goodness. I praise Your mercy, and I give thanks for Your boundless love.

True Devotion: Nos. 243-254

Those who undertake this holy slavery should have a special devotion to the great mystery of the Incarnation of the Word (25th March). Indeed, the Incarnation is the mystery proper in this practice, inasmuch as it is a devotion inspired by the Holy Ghost; first to honor and imitate the ineffable dependence which God the Son was pleased to have on Mary, for His Father's glory – and our salvation – which dependence particularly appears in this mystery where Jesus is a captive and a slave in the bosom of his Blessed Mother, and depends on her for all things. Secondly, to thank God for the incomparable graces He has given Mary and particularly for having chosen her to be His most holy Mother, which choice was made in this mystery. These are

71

the two principal ends of the slavery of Jesus and
Mary. Because we are living in an age of intellectual
pride and there are around us numerous, puffed-up
scholars, conceited with critical spirit who have
plenty to say against the best established and most
solid practices of piety, it is better for us not to give
them any needless occasion of criticism, hence, it is
better to say, we are slaves of Jesus in Mary and call
ourselves slaves of Jesus Christ, rather than the
slaves of Mary; taking the denomination of our
devotion rather from its last end, which is Jesus
Christ, than from the means to the end, which is
Mary; we may use either term though. Another reason is that the principal mystery we celebrate and
honor in this devotion is the mystery of the
Incarnation wherein we can see Jesus only in Mary,
and incarnate in her bosom. Hence it is more to the
purpose to speak of the slavery of Jesus in Mary, and
of Jesus residing and reigning in Mary according to
that beautiful prayer, "O Jesus Living in Mary", etc.

Those who adopt this slavery ought to have a
great devotion to saying the Hail Mary. Few
Christians, however enlightened, know the real
value, merit, excellence and necessity of the Hail
Mary. It was necessary for the Blessed Virgin to
appear several times to great and enlightened saints
to show them the merit of it.

Now turn to page 56, For Prayers, etc.

THIRTY-SECOND DAY

Imitation: Book 2, Chapter 7

Of Loving Jesus Above All Things

Blessed is the man who knows what it is to love Jesus, and to despise himself for the sake of Jesus. You must give up all other love for His, since He wishes to be loved alone above all.

Love of creatures is deceiving and constantly changing, but the love of Jesus is true and permanent. If you hold on to creatures, you will fall with them; if you hold on to Jesus, you will remain firmly planted forever.

Love Him then keep Him as a friend. He will not leave you as others do; nor will He permit you to suffer eternal death. Separate yourself a little from everything, then. Cling, therefore to Jesus in life and death; trust yourself to Him alone who can help you when all others fail you.

The nature of Christ's love is such that it will not admit a rival; He wants you for Himself alone. He desires to sit on the throne of your heart as King; which is His right. If you only knew how to free yourself of the love of creatures, how quickly would He come into your heart!

True Devotion: Nos. 257-260

There are also some very sanctifying interior practices for those whom the Holy Ghost calls to a high perfection. These may be expressed in four words: to do all our actions: by Mary, with Mary, in

Mary, and for Mary, so that we may do them all the more perfectly by Jesus, with Jesus, in Jesus and for Jesus.

By Mary: We must obey her in all things, in all things conduct ourselves by her spirit which is the Holy spirit of God "those who are led by the Spirit of God, are the children of God." Those who are led by the spirit of Mary, are the children of Mary, and among the clients of Mary, none are true or faithful but those who are led by her spirit. Jesus has rendered Himself, so completely the Master of Mary, that He has become her own spirit. A soul is happy indeed when it is all possessed and overruled by the spirit of Mary, a spirit meek and strong, zealous and prudent,humble and courageous, pure and fruitful.

We must do our actions *with Mary.* We must consider in every action how Mary has done it, she being in our place. For this end, we must meditate on the great virtues which she practiced during her life, first of all her lively faith, by which she believed, without hesitation, the angel's word, and believed faithfully and constantly, up to the foot of the Cross; her profound humility which made her hide herself, hold her peace, submit to everything, and put herself last of all.

Now turn to page 56, For Prayers, etc.

THIRTY-THIRD DAY

Imitation: Book 4, Chapter 11

Of The Necessity Of Communion

O sweetest Lord Jesus, how happy is the devout man who feasts at Your banquet, at which there is no other food but Yourself, his only Lover, most desired of all that his heart can desire!

How deeply I long to pour out my heartfelt tears in Your presence, and like the pious Magdalen, to wash Your feet with them. But where is such devotion in me, such copious shedding of holy tears? Surely, in Your sight, and before Your holy angels, my whole heart ought to be inflamed and weep for joy; for I have You with me truly present in this Sacrament, though You are under another form. My eyes could not bear to see You in Your own divine brightness, nor could the whole world stand in sight of the splendor of Your majesty. In concealing Yourself in this Sacrament You have regard for my weakness.

True Devotion: Nos. 261-265

We must do our actions *in Mary.* Our Blessed Lady is the true terrestrial paradise of the New Adam, and the ancient paradise was but a figure of her. In this earthly paradise we have riches, beauties, rarities and inexplicable sweetness, which Jesus Christ, the New Adam has left here; it was in this paradise that He took His complacence for nine months, worked His wonders and displayed His riches with the mag-

nificence of a God. It is in this earthly paradise that
there is the true tree of life, which has borne Jesus
Christ, the Fruit of Life, and the tree of knowledge of
good and evil, which has given light unto the world.
There are, in this divine place, trees planted by the
hand of God, and watered by His Divine Unction,
which have borne and daily bear fruit of divine taste.
It is only the Holy Ghost, Who can make us know
the hidden truth of these figures of material things.
The Holy Ghost, by the mouth of the Fathers, also
styles the Blessed Virgin the Eastern Gate, by which
the High-Priest, Jesus Christ, enters the world, and
leaves it. By it, He came the first time, He will come
the second, by it.

Finally, we must do all our actions *for Mary*, we
must take her for our proximate end, our mysterious
means, and our way to go to Jesus Christ. Supported
by her protection we must undertake and achieve
great things for Christ. We must defend her privileges, when they are disputed. We must stand up for
her glory when it is attacked; we must draw all the
world, if we can, to her service, and to this true and
solid devotion. We must pretend to no recompense
for our little service, except the honor of belonging to
so sweet a Queen, and the happiness of being united
through her to Jesus, her Son, by an indissoluble tie,
in time and in eternity.

Now turn to page 56, For Prayers, etc.

True Devotion: Nos. 231-233
How to Make Your Consecration

At the end of three weeks, we should go to Confession and Holy Communion with the intention of giving ourselves to Jesus Christ in the quality of slaves of love, by the hands of Mary. After Communion, we should recite the consecration prayer; we ought to write it, or have it written, and sign it the same day the consecration is made. It would be well that on this day, we should pay some tribute to Jesus Christ and our Blessed Lady, either as a penance for our past unfaithfulness to the vows of Baptism, or as a testimony of dependence on the dominion of Jesus and Mary. This tribute should be one in accordance with your fervor, such as a fast, a mortification or an alms, or a candle. If but a pin is given in homage, and given with a good heart, it will be enough for Jesus, Who loves only the good will.

Once a year at least, and on the same day, we should renew this consecration, observing the same practices during the three weeks.

Consecration of oneself to Jesus Christ, Wisdom incarnate, through the hands of Mary

ternal and incarnate Wisdom, most lovable and adorable Jesus, true God and true man, only Son of the eternal Father and of Mary always Virgin, I adore you profoundly, dwelling in the splendor of your Father from all eternity, and in the virginal womb of Mary, your most worthy Mother, at the time of your Incarnation.

I thank you for having emptied yourself in assuming the condition of a slave to set me free from the cruel slavery of the evil one.

I praise and glorify you for having willingly chosen to obey Mary, your holy Mother, in all things, so that through her I may be your faithful slave of love.

But I must confess that I have not kept the vows and promises which I made to you so solemnly at my baptism. I have not fulfilled my obligations, and I do not deserve to be called your child or even your slave.

Since I cannot lay claim to anything except what merits your rejection and displeasure, I dare no longer approach the holiness of your majesty on my own. That is why I turn to the intercession and the mercy of your holy Mother, whom you yourself have given me to mediate with you. Through her I hope to obtain

78

from you contrition and pardon for my sins, and that Wisdom whom I desire to dwell in me always.

I turn to you, then, Mary immaculate, living tabernacle of God, in whom Eternal Wisdom willed to receive the adoration of both men and angels.

I greet you as Queen of heaven and earth, for all that is under God has been made subject to your sovereignty.

I call upon you, the unfailing refuge of sinners, confident in your mercy that has never forsaken anyone.

Grant my desire for divine Wisdom and, in support of my petition, accept the promises and the offering of myself which I now make, conscious of my unworthiness.

I, an unfaithful sinner, renew and ratify today through you my baptismal promises. I renounce forever Satan, his empty promises, and his evil designs, and I give myself completely to Jesus Christ, the incarnate Wisdom, to carry my cross after him for the rest of my life, and to be more faithful to him than I have been till now.

This day, with the whole court of heaven as witness, I choose you, Mary, as my Mother and Queen. I surrender and consecrate myself to you, body and soul, as your slave, with all that I possess, both spiritual and material, even including the value of all my good actions, past, present, and to come. I give you the full right to dispose of me and all that belongs to me, without any reservations, in whatever way you please, for the greater glory of God in time and throughout eternity.

Accept, gracious Virgin, this little offering of my slavery to honor and imitate the obedience which Eternal Wisdom willingly chose to have towards you, his Mother. I wish to acknowledge the authority which both of you have over this pitiful sinner. By it, I wish also to thank God for the privileges bestowed on you by the Blessed Trinity. I declare that for the future, I will try to honor and obey you in all things, as your true slave of love.

O admirable Mother, present me to your dear Son as his slave, now and for always, so that he who redeemed me through you, will now receive me through you.

Mother of mercy, grant me the favor of obtaining the true Wisdom of God, and so make me one of those whom you love, teach and guide, whom you nourish and protect as your children and slaves.

Virgin most faithful, make me in everything so committed a disciple, imitator, and slave of Jesus, your Son, incarnate Wisdom, that I may become, through your intercession and example, fully mature with the fullness which Jesus possessed on earth, and with the fullness of his glory in heaven. Amen.

_____
Sign your name here

Date_____

Montfort Publications - Bay Shore, N.Y. 11706-8993

Cum approbatione ecclesiastica.

Confraternity of Mary, Queen of All Hearts

Once you have made your consecration, it is recommended that you join the *Confraternity of Mary, Queen of All Hearts*.

1. *Nature and purpose of the Confraternity.*

The Confraternity of Mary, Queen of All Hearts, is a pious union of the faithful, without officers or meetings. Its purpose is to help the members live and publicize the Marian Way of Life as the easier and more secure means to sanctify themselves.

2. *How to join the Confraternity.*

"Membership in the Confraternity is acquired by entering the applicant's name in the official register" of any Confraternity Center. *(One such Confraternity is directed by:* The Montfort Fathers, Bay Shore, New York)

3. *Conditions for Membership.*

a. "Any Catholic, including clerics and religious, may become a member of the Confraternity of Mary, Queen of All Hearts . . . the members may assume other obligations special to their spiritual life or their apostolate. b. Prior to their enrollment, the applicants must consecrate themselves to the Blessed Virgin, using for this purpose the consecration of St. Louis Marie De Montfort."
(Rescript, July 16, 1955).

4. *Obligations*

In keeping with the purpose of the Confraternity, the members should enrich their lives with a Marian spirit – doing all things with Mary, through Mary, in Mary, and for Mary. By this means, they will more perfectly live and act with, through, in, and for Christ.

They should renew their consecration faithfully and frequently, making a special practice of renewing it every morning at the beginning of each new day.

Share in Good Works

The members share in all the good works and prayers of the members of the Company of Mary and the Daughters of Wisdom.

Feasts of the Confraternity

The Annunciation (March 25) is the principal feast of the Confraternity. On this feast, there is recalled to our minds the great truth of Our Divine Lord's Incarnation and that He came to us through Mary and willed to submit Himself to her, His Holy Mother.

The feast of Saint Louis De Montfort (April 28) is the second principal feast of the Confraternity.

Other special feasts of the Confraternity are: the Immaculate Conception (December 8), Christmas (December 25), the Purification (February 2), the Visitation (May 31), the Assumption (August 15), the Immaculate Heart of Mary, the feast of our Lady of Sorrows (September 15).

INDULGENCES

On the occasion of the initial consecration (using the De Montfort formula) or, on the occasion of its renewal, a PLENARY INDULGENCE is granted, under the usual conditions (Confession, Communion and prayer for the intentions of the Holy Father). Also, a PLENARY INDULGENCE on the following days: 1 - The day of enrollment in the Confraternity; 2 - Holy Thursday; 3 - Christmas; 4 - Feast of the Annunciation; 5 - Feast of the Immaculate Conception; (Dec. 8); 6 - St. Louis De Montfort's Feast day (April 28); 7 - Every First Saturday of the Month.

Members of the Confraternity also share in the satisfaction, prayers and good works of the Missionaries of the Company of Mary (the Montfort Fathers and Brothers), the Daughters of Wisdom, and the Brothers of St. Gabriel, the three congregations founded by St. Louis De Montfort.

In answer to a petition by the Montfort Missionaries to the Sacred Penitentiary in Rome, the above Indulgences have now been granted in perpetuity to the two Confraternities *(Priests of Mary, Queen of All Hearts and the Confraternity of Mary, Queen of All Hearts)*, thus bringing them in line with the conditions laid down by the new *Enchiridion* of Indulgences.

If you wish to be enrolled in the Confraternity of Mary Queen of All Hearts, send your name and address to the nearest Confraternity or to:

THE MONTFORT MISSIONARIES
Queen of All Hearts Confraternity
Bay Shore, New York 11706-8993

God alone
The Collected Writings of Saint Louis Marie de Montfort

672 pages, with introductions, guides
and indexes. Well printed on smooth,
durable paper. Illustrations and color
to add to the book's attractiveness. A
fine blue binding, with gilt stamping
and highly glossy gilt edges to the
pages. Multi-colored, lacquered, durable
jacket. Order from:

Montfort Publications
Bay Shore, N.Y. 11706-8993